FESTIVAL

Carnival

Olivia Bennett

Contents

…tute was opened in …nderstanding of the …ne Commonwealth, through education, exhibitions and the arts.

Education programmes have been offered to well over 100 000 children at the Institute each year and many more are reached through extramural programmes and publications.

In pursuing its objectives, the Institute has been responsible for a number of new initiatives, none of which has been more rewarding than its Festivals programmes for schools, which enable many hundreds of children to participate in the celebration of some of the Commonwealth's most significant cultural events. We feel strongly that this opportunity should be offered more widely to teachers and children and are delighted to be able to share in this venture with Macmillan. We trust that this publication will be of assistance to those wanting to know more about Britain's increasingly multicultural society and the wider world in which we live.

James Porter

Director of the Commonwealth Institute

M
MACMILLAN
EDUCATION

Carnival in Trinidad

▼ During Carnival the streets of Trinidad's capital, Port-of-Spain, are full of masqueraders dressed in colourful costumes.

It is Carnival time in Trinidad. The sun is shining, the air is full of music, and everyday life has come to a standstill. But nothing else is standing still! The streets are full of people dancing, singing or playing music.

It is Tuesday, the second day of Carnival. The costume bands form a river of colour through the streets. Each band takes a theme. Its members are divided into groups, in matching fancy dress, who illustrate different parts of the theme. Three groups dressed in dazzling yellow and red pass by. They represent Sunflowers, Flames and Firefighters. Their band's theme is 'Some Like it Hot'. Then a troupe of Dollar Bills parade past, followed by Ten Cents and Small Change. The band's title is 'We Money'.

Band leaders take their ideas from history, current events, legends and their own fantasies. In one day you might see people disguised as Roman emperors and empresses, American soldiers, English Beefeaters, Red Indians, birds of paradise, trees and playing cards.

As the sun goes down, the streets get even more crowded. People shuffle, sway and 'jump up' to the sound of the steelbands. Most Trinidadians celebrate Carnival

▲ Trinidad's steelbands compete with each other to become Band of the Year. They begin rehearsing for Carnival many months before the festival.

▶ If you look closely at this man's head-dress, you will see that the shields and the white masks are based on African tribal designs. They are a reminder that many Trinidadians orginally came from Africa.

without stopping – even for sleep! The musicians, singers and masqueraders in their fancy dress have been planning and practising for months. Some start designing next year's Carnival costumes as soon as they have recovered from the last one!

A story to tell

As well as music and colour, Carnival is full of storytelling. The calypso singers make up songs which comment on people and events. The stories they tell often contain funny, sly or cheeky remarks. Sometimes they contain sad or angry comments about life.

The costume bands bring street theatre to Carnival, with those watching on the sidelines getting caught up in the miming and acting of the masqueraders.

Trinidad and Tobago's festival has its own story to tell too. All the different activities are like pieces in a jigsaw. As we explore the costumes and the calypsoes, the music and masqueraders, and fit the pieces together, we'll find more than a picture of Carnival. We will find that they can tell us a lot about the islands and the history of the Trinidadian people – who have made Carnival one of the world's greatest festivals.

▼ Carnival is the biggest event of the year in Trinidad and Tobago. There are newspaper articles about it for months before and after the festival.

EXPRESS Monday February 21, 1983

'COMMITTEE OF 10' ONE OF THE TRIUMPHS OF CARNIVAL '83

THIEF WARRIOR GLADIATOR KING

EXPRESS Friday, February 11, 1983

CARNIVAL'S MIXTURE OF MADNESS, GLADNESS AND HARDNESS HAS ONCE MORE PROVED TOO RICH FOR THE CDC'S JUDGES

Just look at the kaiso crop for Sunday night

EXPRESS Sunday February, 20, 1983

VICTORIA SQUARE MAS RESULTS

Showcase wins Downtown prize

its BRass STeel & Calypso

NEW CARNIVAL CITY

CHACACABANA CHAGUARAMAS

Trinidad Troubadors

Cossoks with Brass

Errol Ince Vibrations

Music Makers

Lord Nelson

Kings, Queens on stage again tonight

In South 3 bands grab 6 places

Lifestyle

CARNIVAL IS COLOUR, AS WELL AS CONTROVERSY

BY ANTHONY MILNE

Feast before fast

The biggest celebrations take place in Trinidad and Tobago's capital, Port-of-Spain. Carnival takes place on the Monday and Tuesday before Ash Wednesday, which is the first day of Lent. Lent is the name given to the forty days before the important Christian festival of Easter. It is a thoughtful time for Christians, when they traditionally fasted and gave up any sort of merry-making. So the last few days before Lent were often marked by wild feasts and celebrations, particularly in Catholic countries. In fact, it was Catholic Europeans who first brought Carnival to Trinidad.

Preparations

The excitement of Carnival starts building up long before the festivities take place. There are lots of parties. From New Year's Eve onwards, the calypso singers and steelbands start composing and playing together in halls or practice rooms known as 'tents'. Each one wants to keep their ideas and tunes secret from the other bands. As a band may have more than 25 people hammering out the melody, keeping it a surprise isn't always easy.

▼ The weeks of competitions, parades and events before Carnival add to the growing excitement.

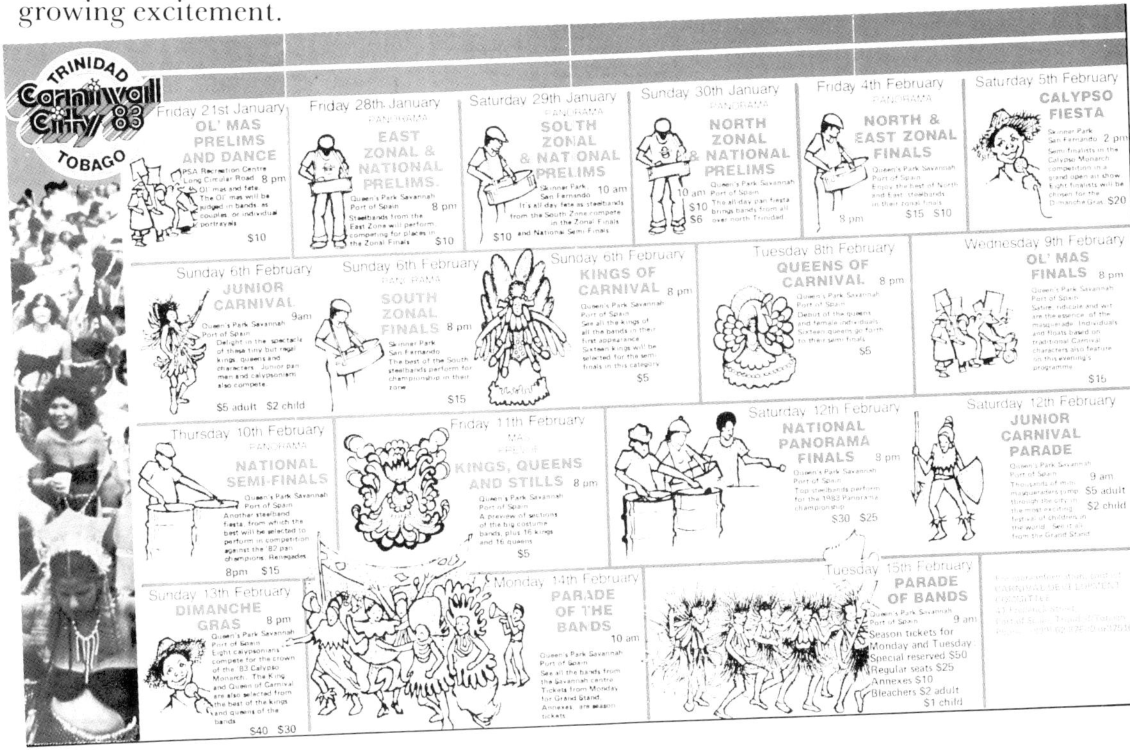

Even before the tents are in full swing, the leaders of the costume bands are looking over designs and ideas. As Carnival gets closer, their preparations get more hectic. Coloured and shiny materials, sequins, glitter, feathers, glue, cotton thread, tissue paper, beads and paint disappear from the shops into people's homes and the workshops known as 'mas camps'.

Competitions

In the days before Carnival opens there are many semi-finals of the competitions to find the best musicians, singers and masqueraders. Hundreds of children take part in the Junior Carnival too.

On the Sunday, known as Dimanche Gras, the King and Queen of Carnival are crowned. At 4 o'clock the next morning a rocket goes off to announce the start of Carnival – but hardly anyone has gone to bed anyway! Its J'Ouvert, or Jouvay, as many Trinidadians call it. People dress up in their old Carnival costumes and join in the Ol' Mas fun. A day and night of dancing and music follows. On Tuesday the costume bands take over the streets. Rum, fruit juice and sweet and spicy snacks keep the dancers, singers and masqueraders going, right until the 'las lap' and the midnight hour. Suddenly it's Ash Wednesday and Carnival is over for another year.

The history of Carnival

Christopher Columbus arrived in Trinidad in 1498. He claimed it for Spain, although it was nearly a hundred years before any Spaniards settled there. ▶

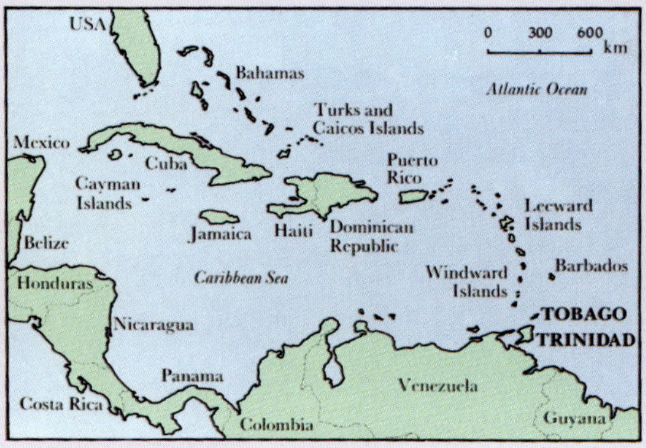

◀ Trinidad and Tobago lie in the south-east corner of the Caribbean sea. Spanish settlers first grew tobacco and cocoa on the island's rich tropical soil, but it was sugar which brought the colony prosperity.

'Dimanche Gras', 'J' Ouvert', 'Ol Mas', 'Carnival'. All these words contain clues about the story of the festival and of Trinidad and Tobago. Carnival comes from the latin 'carne vale'. This means 'farewell to flesh'. Many Christians gave up meat or sweet things during Lent, as well as 'sins of the flesh' such as over-eating and wild singing and dancing. 'Dimanche' is Sunday in French. Playing 'mas' and 'Ol Mas' come from 'masquerade', the French word for masked balls. 'Jouvay' or 'J' Ouvert' comes from 'le jour est ouvert' which means 'the day is open' in French – it is daybreak, and Carnival has begun! All these different pieces of the jigsaw fit together when you remember that the first people to celebrate Carnival and play mas in Trinidad were French Catholic plantation owners.

The melting pot

In Trinidad and Tobago today, you'll find people descended from those French Catholics, as well as from the English, Spanish, Chinese, Venezuelans, Americans, Dutch, Lebanese and Syrians who have settled in the islands over the last 300 or so years. Above all, you'll find Trinidadians descended from the Africans and East Indians who worked on the plantations and who today form most of the population. And it is they who have made most mark on Carnival celebrations. For the story of Carnival may have started with the

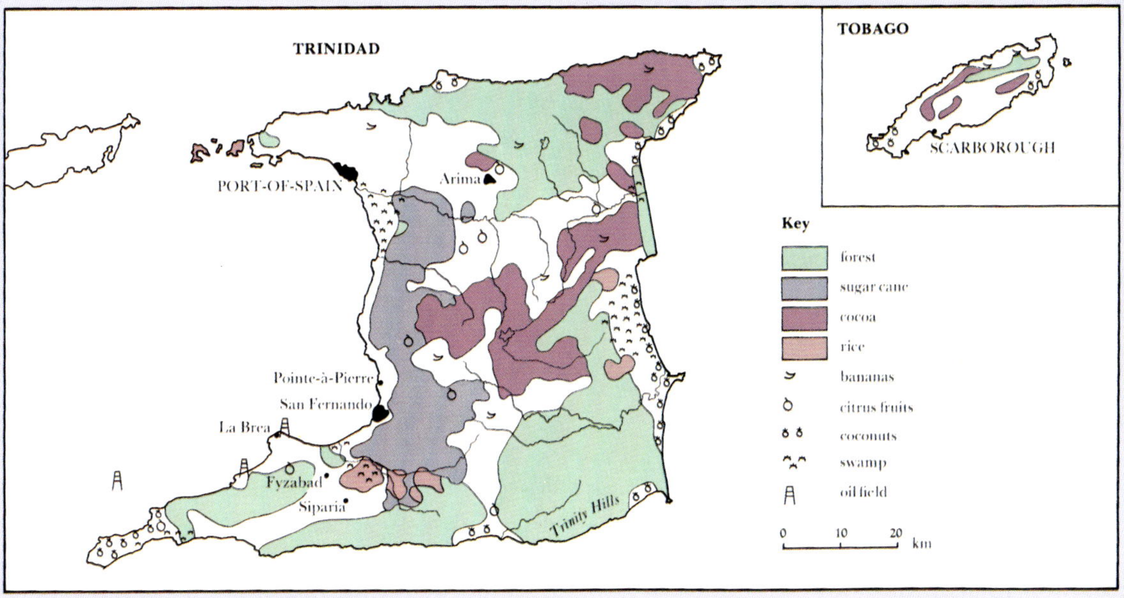

French, but the way it has developed is the result of Trinidad's many races bringing their own music, dance, drama and storytelling to it.

Many races, one nation

Many things about Trinidad remind you of the way many different cultures live together there. You'll see Christian churches, Hindu and Chinese temples, Jewish synagogues and Muslim mosques. As well as English, you'll hear mixtures of French and Spanish, and words and phrases from Hindi and African languages in people's speech. Place names tell the same story. The French Pointe-à-Pierre, English Scarborough, Spanish San Fernando, and Hindi Fyzabad are just some you can find on the map. And names like Arima and Siparia come from the very first inhabitants of the country, the Amerindian Arawaks and Caribs.

Christopher Columbus reached the Amerindians' island and claimed it for Spain in 1498. The Spanish settlers were fairly poor and had to fight off raids by Dutch, French and English. From 1793 Spain encouraged Catholics of any nationality to move there. Many French settlers came. They started to grow sugar cane and soon they were making lots of money.

Slaves and settlers

It was these French settlers who spent some of their new wealth on masked balls, street parades and festivities before the fasting of Lent. Their African slaves were not allowed to join in the celebrations or even to make their own music with their drums.

In 1797 the British captured Trinidad. More French, Spanish and English-speaking settlers made it their home. The flow of slave labour continued, but in 1833 slavery was abolished. Carnival became the ideal time for the free slaves to show their love of music, dance and celebration. They turned the upper class Carnival into a lively folk festival. They brought their once-forbidden drumming, and the music and dance of Africa out into the streets.

Alarmed by this, the landowners and gentry took their festivities away from the streets and into their homes. They also began to look around for another source of cheap labour to care for the precious sugar crop from which their money came. They found it in India, where there were many people in need of work. The life of the East Indians in Trinidad was hard but, unlike the former slaves, they were allowed to keep their religion and customs. They too brought great skill at drumming and dancing, and festivals in which shrines and religious figures were paraded through the streets. These

◀ Trinidadians are a mixture of many races and colours. Descendants of European settlers and the Africans, Indians and Chinese who worked on the land, today live and work together to give Trinidad a particularly rich and lively culture, of which Carnival is its best expression.

▶ Harvesting coconuts. The dried flesh, which is called copra, is used to make oil and soap. Other important crops in Trinidad are cocoa, citrus fruits, bananas and coffee.

East Indians added much to the Carnival tradition of designing dazzling masks, head-dresses and moving floats.

As Carnival became wilder and more popular, the authorities became more worried about it. Some feared that the wearing of masks might allow crime and violence to take place. Others were frightened by the powerful drumming and the possibility of rebellion by the poor. Over the years, the authorities banned certain activities – but they couldn't kill Carnival. In fact, each ban just encouraged new ways of celebration.

When drumming was banned, Tamboo Bamboo bands were set up to make music. False beards and face paint took the place of masks. The total ban on Carnival during World War Two led to music-making experiments on junk and scrap materials. The result was that when peace came, Carnival burst on to the streets with a more lively sound than ever before – steelband music!

Carnival today combines all the different ingredients Trinidadians have added to it during their history. It is now the most important event in their year and it is enjoyed by every part of Trinidad's society, whatever their colour, religion or background.

Trinidad today

▶ The oil refinery at Pointe-à-Pierre is one of the biggest in the world. Oil has played its own part in the story of Carnival too. Experiments on old oil drums led to the development of steelbands and pan music.

▶▶ Pitch lake, La Brea. Sir Walter Raleigh stopped at Trinidad on his search for El Dorado. He patched up his leaking ships with the thick sticky asphalt which still oozes out of the ground at La Brea today, and which has been exported all over the world.

◀ Sugar cane being harvested. The money to be made from sugar attracted European settlers to Trinidad. French Catholic plantation owners first brought Carnival celebrations to the islands at the end of the eighteenth century.

So Carnival owes its excitement, colour and music to the many different races who have made Trinidad and Tobago their home. And the crop that first drew them there was sugar. The French and other Europeans came to make money from it. The Africans were brought to care for it. Once they had gained their freedom, the East Indians, Chinese and others came to take their place in the cane fields. Today sugar is still grown but it is no longer such a money-spinner for Trinidad. It remains an important crop in the Caribbean region, however.

Towards the end of the eighteenth century cocoa became more important to farmers than sugar. Then, in the 1920s, it became more difficult to make money from cocoa too. Luckily for Trinidad, oil had been discovered. The new industry soon started to make money. It has made Trinidad the richest of the Caribbean countries.

Oil, however, cannot supply all the country's needs. The rock structures in which it is trapped make it difficult and expensive to get out. Experts think that supplies may run out by the end of the

century. Although the industry makes a lot of money, it does not provide a lot of jobs, and many Trinidadians are looking for work.

Changes

Most working Trinidadians have jobs in farming and forestry. Some work in the factories of the small industries which the Government is encouraging. Natural gas is a growing industry. The pitch lake where Sir Walter Raleigh mended his leaking ships hundreds of years ago, still produces more asphalt than anywhere else in the world. As Trinidad's population grows, however, farmland is covered up by houses and villages. Work becomes more difficult to find. Although Trinidad's early history is as a land where people came to find work and money, for some years now its people have been leaving the islands to find jobs in Britain, North America and elsewhere. Wherever they go, they take the gaiety and excitement of Carnival with them. Wherever there are Trinidadians, there are Carnival celebrations. As they say, 'Our greatest exports are oil and Carnival'.

Playing Mas

Carnival itself is really a Trinidadian industry. Each year, people spend thousands of working hours and dollars producing this spectacular show. Some people feel that it is a waste that so much effort and skill goes towards a few days of splendour and excitement, after which the brilliant costumes are not seen again. Trinidadians are exploring the chances of setting up small industries to make the millions of sequins, miles of gold lamé and other materials which are brought into the country each year for the masqueraders.

The costumes which are the result of all this work can – and do – represent just about anything you think of. Each year there is a mixture of old and new ideas. Some traditional characters, like the ones on these pages, almost always appear. They too are pieces in the jigsaw picture of Carnival.

Traditional characters

In the days when Carnival was only enjoyed by the rich, some of their masquerades involved dressing up to look like their African slaves and dancing to drums. Pierrots, minstrels, clowns, jesters and robbers were other popular disguises.

When slavery was stopped and the Africans were free to join in the celebrations, they added their own traditional characters to the parades. They also took the chance to dress up as their former masters and make fun of them. Later, this kind of mockery was used against lawyers, politicians and other people in authority. It is still part of Carnival fun today, especially on J' Ouvert.

Moco Jumbie was a traditional West African character. He became a favourite Carnival disguise, bobbing along the streets on tall stilts.

Jab Molassi is always popular. Jab comes from the French word for devil, 'diable'. Molassi comes from molasses, a dark treacly syrup made from sugar. Jab Molassi darts about, swishing his devil's tail and threatening to smear the crowd with the sticky molasses which covers him from head to foot.

Burroquite is a mixture of East Indian, Spanish and South American ideas. Burro is Spanish for donkey. The wearer of this costume looks as though he or she is riding one.

There are always plenty of **Wild Indians** in the Carnival crowds. These were first based on Amerindians from Venezuela who used to trade in Trinidad more than 100 years ago. They often look more like characters out of American wild west films now. Wild Indians shout fierce war cries and are meant to be violent and thoughtless characters. Because of this, they have been used to poke fun at politicians, for example, by suggesting that they behave the same way.

Canbouley

Another Carnival tradition which tells us about Trinidad's history is Canbouley. This street procession with flaming torches, stick fights, drumming, dancing and singing copies the huge freedom marches which took place every August after the ending of slavery. Canbouley comes from 'cannes brulées', which is French for burnt (sugar) canes. Whenever fires broke out on the plantations, slaves from neighbouring farms were rounded up to fight the fire and cut the cane. Canbouley became a symbol of freedom for the Africans and after a while it became part of the Carnival celebrations.

Costume bands

Carnival Tuesday, sometimes called Mardi Gras, is the day when the costume bands fill the streets. There may be anything from 400 to 2000 people in a band, although some have as many as 4000 masqueraders and musicians. Bands compete fiercely with each other to dream up the cleverest themes and make the most magnificent costumes. The best ones turn the streets of Port-of-Spain into a living theatre.

The search for new themes starts soon after the end of the last Carnival. Once an idea has been decided upon, there is a lot of work to be done on the costume designs.

◀◀ This masquerader is dressed as Lady Luck. Sometimes a costume is so elaborate that the wearer has to use wheels to support part of it!

◀ Costume bands may have 2000 or more members. They often carry brilliantly coloured banners, flags or umbrellas to add to the size, movement and effect of the band.

▶ Hundreds of children take part in Junior Carnival. They are beginning to rival their parents with the brilliance of their costumes!

It is a real art to find and work with materials which are strong, yet light enough not to weigh down somebody wearing an elaborate costume! Band leaders like to keep their ideas to themselves and their supporters. All dream of winning the prize 'Band of the Year'.

Many themes are historical, such as 'The Incas' or 'Ancient Romans'. Others explore something like the creatures of the sea, pieces on a chessboard or the flags of the Commonwealth. Bands may illustrate recent events, perhaps in politics or show business. In fact, costume bands can portray anything from an unpopular government to a popular film.

Junior Carnival

Trinidad's children do more than just join in the grown-ups' fun. They have their own Carnival. The schools form their own steelbands and write their own calypsoes. Teachers, parents and grandparents all help create costumes on themes such as nursery rhymes, 'The Arabian Nights', 'The Kingdom of Snow and Ice' and 'Merrie England'. They have illustrated their fantasies about food and their own ideas such as 'Don't spread litter'. Junior Carnival is full of glitter, fun and laughter and has become very popular.

The story of the Steelband

▲ Tuning a steel pan by tapping up the notes on the drum's surface is a very skilled job.

▲ A Tamboo Bamboo band.

It is not often that a completely new musical sound is invented – but the people of Trinidad did just that when they started playing the first steel pans. If you have ever heard a steelband play, you will know how lively and melodic it sounds. The notes seem to ripple and slide into each other. Usually they make you want to jump up and dance. A steelband can play anything from calypso songs to classical symphonies. And all this music first came from rusty old oil drums!

The drums are called pans. Each section that you see on the surface of the drum plays a different note. The sections playing the highest notes are sunk the deepest. Beating out the pans and tuning them is a very skilled job.

Pan music grew out of the Trinidadians' love of music which, as you'll discover, just could not be stopped – whether there were instruments to play or not! To find out how it developed, we need to look back at the history of Trinidad again.

▼ Tamboo Bamboo instruments.
The **foulé** gives out the high notes. One of the joints in the stem is kept intact.
The **cutter** is usually beaten with a stick. A hole is made through the second joint, but the bottom one is kept intact.
The **boom** has three joints. The bottom one is left intact. It is thumped on the ground to give the basic rhythm.

Foulé
light
bamboo

Cutter
medium
bamboo

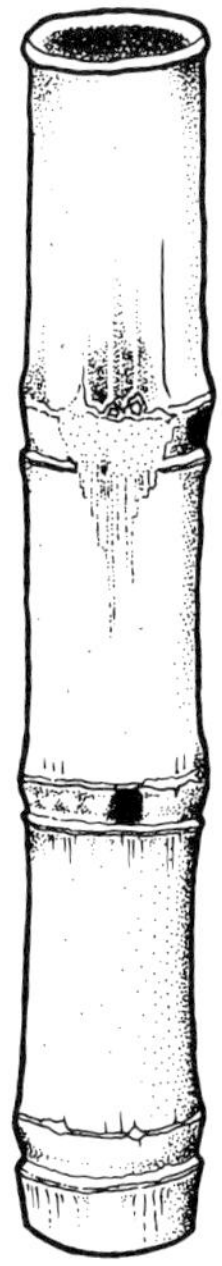

Boom
heavy
bamboo

Tamboo Bamboo Bands

The Africans brought to work on Trinidad's land were very good drummers. When these slaves were freed in 1833, their place was taken by thousands of Indian workers. They, too, brought their own music and drums.

However, the plantation owners and the islands' rulers were not happy with the people's way of making music and celebrating. Some even feared they might use the drums to send secret messages to each other and stir up rebellion. In 1883 they banned the drumming.

Nothing could stop the people from making music, however. Soon they began to make themselves cheap instruments from bamboo stems of different lengths and widths. They thumped them on the ground and played them with sticks in groups called Tamboo Bamboo Bands. Sometimes they added instruments such as a bottle half-full of water and hit it with a spoon. They never stopped trying out new ways of making music. Dustbins, paint cans, biscuit tins, old hubcaps and petrol tanks are some of the things they used. The authorities tried to stop this music too but it was played at Carnival and all over the islands for many years.

The ring of metal music

Throughout the Second World War, Carnival was banned. Trinidad's disappointed musicians continued to experiment with new sounds and instruments, using whatever scrap they could find. When victory came, delighted people spilled on to the streets, playing metal containers of all shapes and sizes and celebrating the end of war – and of five years' without playing mas! As they beat out rhythms on metal pans, cans, and drums, the sound of 'pan' was born.

People first made melodies by simply hitting the tins and oil drums with bits of iron, bottles or spoons. Then the musicians began to 'tune' the pans. By dividing the surface into different notes, separated by deep lines or grooves, they produced instruments capable of many different sounds.

Oil drums make very good pans. Usually the bottom is cut off and the top stretched and beaten so that it curves inwards. The different notes are marked out, and the grooves between them made with a hammer and chisel. Then the metal is heated and quickly cooled to harden it. When cool, the tuner gets to work. He needs a good ear and plenty of patience. The surface of each note is beaten upwards and raised so that exactly the right tone is reached. Finally the drum is cleaned and painted.

◀ The sound of steelbands parading through the streets is one of the most exciting sounds of Carnival. The musicians wheel their drums along the ground on special trolleys.

▼ Calypso singers practise hard, hoping to win the title of Calypso Monarch.

▲ Junior Carnival has steelband competitions too. The children compose their own calypsoes and many schools have their own steelbands.

The first pans were tied round people's necks. Then trolleys and stands were made. During Carnival the drums are played and paraded through the streets on wheels.

As the steel pans improved, bands began to develop their own special sounds and styles. Rivalries developed between them and sometimes fights broke out. At first the authorities looked down on them as 'gutter musicians'. Before long, however, they realised the importance and beauty of this new musical sound. Local firms helped the bands with their costs and today they are invited to play all over the world.

A band can have 25 to 80 members but many get larger at Carnival time. Few players can read music but play by ear and learn each note by heart. They use different sizes of drum to provide the melody, the rhythm and the harmony. Tenor, bass, cello and guitar pans are just some of them. The ping-pong is another. It can produce 32 different notes!

Because a whole band can produce so many different notes, they can play complicated classics as well as simple dance music. Pan is above all, however, a lively sound which just seems to bubble out of the instruments.

The Calypso

By now you have probably got the feeling that Carnival is loud, fun, colourful and musical. As well as the steelband, there is another very special Carnival musical sound – the calypso.

The calypso rhythm is catchy and easy to remember. The words are sharp, witty, often scornful, sometimes sad, and usually full of puns and jokes against the subject of the song. Most have about four verses and a chorus, which the audience may join in.

Nobody can say exactly where the word 'calypso' comes from. Many feel it is from the West African 'kaiso' which means 'bravo – well done'. Certainly, the early slaves used their sense of rhythm and quick wit to make up songs of praise and scorn, which often called for people to join in a chorus. Plantation work songs also made use of African singing styles and rhythms. There are some other kinds of song which may have played a part in the history of the calypso. These are the Amerindian 'carieto', the South American 'caliso' and the French 'carrousseaux'.

◀ Calypso singers often have wierd and wonderful names such as Attila the Hun, and the Mighty Sparrow. This calypsonian, called Crazy, is very popular and has been invited to sing in many countries outside Trinidad.

▶ This verse from a calypso song called 'Capitalism gone mad' sung by the Mighty Sparrow in 1982, is a comment on the high price of goods in Trinidad at that time.

To provide for your family on your present salary
Is impossible, in this country.
So many bills to pay
There is no conceivable way to save for a rainy day
In this country. Is why every damn thing so over priced –
Big business making everybody feel
Government giving them an open license to steal.

However it developed, the calypso today is truly Trinidadian. It is popular in the rest of the Caribbean and all over the world but calypsonians living abroad always try to return to Trinidad for the Carnival competitions.

Calypsonians sing about every aspect of people's lives. Favourite themes are love and marriage, high society, scandal, politics and world events. Nothing is sacred, not even royalty or religion! More than one local politician has been mocked by having his mistakes or broken promises pointed out to the public in a clever and cheeky calypso.

The tents

From the beginning of the year, singers and their musicians organise themselves into practice halls called tents, where they compose and work on the year's selection of songs. The tents draw huge crowds of people every night. A good song is greeted with shouts of 'Kaiso!' A bad one is slow hand-clapped. Judges come to select semi-finalists from the 150 or so calypsonians who hope to be this year's Calypso Monarch. Most of them are men, but there have been some very successful women calypsonians. The catchiest songs are sung by the crowds throughout Carnival. Each year one is picked to be the Carnival theme song, called the Road March.

Changes

▶ Today West Indian communities all over the world hold their own Carnival celebrations, sometimes helped by Trinidad's costume designers and musicians. Costumes like this may now be recreated for another Carnival, instead of being dismantled and never seen again.

Another thing about Carnival which you have probably noticed by now is that, as well as music, it is full of movement. Steelbands parade through the streets, their drums on wheels and trolleys. The costume bands flow through the streets, miming, dancing and singing. The crowds join in and jump up to the sound of pan and calypso. No one stays still. Carnival is like the festival costumes, which come to life when the people within them move and dance. By themselves they are just elaborate constructions of paper, wire, sequins, materials, feathers and paint. It is people who give Carnival its life too.

We have already learnt how it changed and developed with the history of the Trinidadian people. It continues to tell us about them and the rest of the world. If you looked at the words of each year's Road March and favourite calypsoes, you would get a good idea of the events then in the news. Some songs also tell you of the kind of ideas or problems that were on people's minds that year.

The movement and changes in Carnival never stop. The bands have become much larger. Their costumes have become more elaborate and expensive. Recently one band used costumes and

▼ Trinidad's calypso singers use their songs to make funny and sometimes scornful comments on the world we live in.

▲ Wherever they take place, Carnival celebrations have their own special character. Huge speakers stacked on top of each other to make as much noise as possible are a common sight at London's Notting Hill Carnival, where reggae music is especially popular.

mime to warn people of the dangers of modern living and our dependence on machines. Some people disapproved of this. They felt Carnival should be full of fun with no disturbing ideas.

Another change which some people welcome and others dislike is the new sound of 'soca'. The word comes from 'soul calypso'. It has simpler words and a heavier beat. Some say it is just boring 'party music' but many young people like it. Also, music is more often played through loudspeakers now. It gets more expensive every year for large bands to play live. The sound of pan has changed over the years too. The bands have developed different ways of playing. They can now play almost any style of music, but they have not lost the joyful sound they are famous for.

Carnival today attracts thousands of tourists. And Trinidad's masqueraders and musicians are in demand all over the world. So another change is that Carnival music and costumes are not always forgotten after Ash Wednesday. Some get taken to other West Indian communities to help people play mas at carnivals in Britain, North America and elsewhere.

Carnival in Britain

▶ Steelbands are becoming very popular in Britain, especially in schools. Children who cannot read music but who have a good ear for it, can learn to play pan very quickly.

Since Carnival has always grown and changed with the people who celebrate it, it is not surprising to find that wherever West Indians living abroad have got together and created their own Carnival, the celebrations take on their own special character.

In Britain there are Carnival celebrations in Manchester, Leeds, Birmingham, Bristol and north London's Finsbury Park. Perhaps the most popular and spectacular takes place in Notting Hill. One of the things which gives it a special flavour is that it is more Caribbean than purely Trinidadian. Britain's West Indian community contains many more Jamaicans than Trinidadians. So, for example, much more reggae music than pan music booms through the streets of Notting Hill at Carnival time.

The Caribbean community

During the Second World War, many West Indians worked hard for Britain, both in the armed forces and in British factories. After the war, lack of work in many Caribbean islands forced people to look elsewhere for jobs. Britain had the opposite problem. There was a lot of work to be done to put the country back on its feet, and not enough workers to do it. Some industries, such as London Transport, actually sent officials over to the West Indies to let people know what jobs were available.

Many of the people who came to Britain at this time made it their home. Today about half the Caribbean community are Black Britons born in the United Kingdom. Most of the people who emigrated to Britain were Jamaicans. Another

▲ Black Uhuru performing live. The West Indian community has given British popular music some exciting new sounds, especially reggae.

▼ Members of the British Caribbean community have been very active in social and community work. This is the opening of the Stonebridge Bus Project in North London. An old bus garage has been converted for and by the local Caribbean community into a meeting place and centre where people can learn new skills and crafts.

large group came from Barbados. There were also people from St Vincent, Grenada and many other islands. Trinidad's oil wealth meant that fewer people had to leave the island for work.

The West Indians brought with them many skills and customs. Many of them have become part of the British way of life. Reggae is one of the most popular forms of music in Britain today. People love the sound of steelbands and many schools are teaching their children to play pan and start their own band. West Indians are working more and more in local government, the media and public life. They have made a tremendous contribution to the world of sport, recently producing some of Britain's finest athletes. West Indian warmth and friendliness has meant they have given a lot to certain 'caring' jobs such as nursing and social work, as well as to community life. And each year, the Carnivals they have established have got bigger and better!

▲ Notting Hill Carnival is now so popular that over a quarter of a million people join in the celebrations. The sound of reggae through loudspeakers competes with the music of many steelbands. Some of these come especially from Trinidad.

▼ Notting Hill is not the only community in Britain to have a Carnival. West Indians in Bristol, Birmingham, Manchester and Leeds, as well as London's Finsbury Park, have worked hard to set up similar successful festivals.

Notting Hill Carnival

London's Notting Hill Carnival should not be seen as a small version of Trinidad's Carnival. It is different in many ways and has developed its own character. One of the most obvious differences is that it takes place on a public holiday in August, not just before Lent. A carnival in a British February or March would be a cold and probably wet celebration! The move to the summer ended the link with Lent but made good sense.

The greater number of West Indians from Jamaica and Caribbean islands other than Trinidad means that the sound of the Notting Hill Carnival is more often Jamaican reggae than the sound of a steelband. Less of the music is live, and much is played through stacks of enormous loudspeakers, some the size of wardrobes! Reggae and soca are becoming increasingly popular in Trinidad but the real sound of Carnival to a Trinidadian is still a steelband on wheels parading through the streets.

Another small difference is that in Trinidad nobody stays still and just watches. The crowds are always 'jumping up' and leaving the pavements to take part in the parades. In Notting Hill the pavements are full of people who enjoy watching the action,

▲ In the days before the Notting Hill Carnival takes place, there are competitions and prizes for the best costumes and bands.

although each year more and more people join in the processions.

Finally, it takes place in a small part of London and doesn't take over the city centre in the way that Port-of-Spain gives itself up to Carnival. Carnival is not a national celebration as it is in Trinidad. Although more and more areas in Britain are setting up their own Carnivals, they remain pockets of fun for local communities.

The build-up of months of preparations, competitions, parties, and entertainment in tents is missing too. In spite of this, the music and costumes are very good. And each year there are more events leading up to Carnival-time in Britain.

Notting Hill does have a Junior Carnival. Teachers, pupils and parents spend a lot of time making splendid masquerades for the great day when the children cram on to decorated lorries and parade slowly through the crowded streets.

Mingling with the people are street entertainers of all kinds. There are stalls selling Caribbean and other types of food, souvenirs and masks. Everywhere there is the throbbing beat of music. Some is supplied by Trinidadian calypsonians and musicians, who have come over to add their magic to the Carnival fun.

Carnival in other lands

▶ A Good Friday procession in a Maltese village marks the end of Lent and the beginning of the Easter festival. Carnival in Malta used to take place just before Lent, as it does in Trinidad. It is now celebrated in the warmer month of May, so that the weather is better for the street parades and parties.

Another famous Carnival takes place in Brazil. Most Brazilians are Catholic and Lent comes during their hot summer months. The streets of the main Brazilian cities are full all night of people in fancy dress enjoying the fun of Carnival before Ash Wednesday dawns. Many people just snatch a few hours sleep in the early morning before picking themselves up and swaying to the music of the samba all over again. The rhythmic sound of samba music is what gives Brazil's Carnival its special flavour.

Brazilians, like Trinidadians, are a complete mixture of races and colours. Carnival is most brilliantly celebrated in the northern cities of Salvador and Recife, where many of the descendants of African families live. Much of Brazil's lively music comes from the songs, dances and drumming brought by the Africans to Brazil many years ago.

Rio de Janeiro and São Paulo also have fantastic Carnival celebrations. Many factories and offices close down for the festival. Rio becomes a sort of fantasy city. A visitor may find him or herself standing next to a Wild Indian, with a two metre long feather head-dress, in the queue for a

▼ Carnival in Rio. Carnival in Brazil is famous for the samba dancing. The rhythmic sound of samba was first brought from Africa and has become Brazil's favourite music.

bus! On the bus he or she may come across a group of exhausted dancers in fancy dress, going home to catch a quick breakfast before starting to samba again. Dodging the city traffic in front of the bus there may be someone wheeling home a huge decorated float in order to make some repairs before the processions start again and the streets fill with strutting and swaying bodies.

New Orleans is another city famous for its Mardi Gras celebrations. Again, many of its most lively features have an African history. Many Catholic countries in Europe have exciting Carnivals before Lent. Rome is famous for its festivities. Malta's Carnival celebrations include parades through the streets, fancy dress balls and dancing competitions.

Carnival is now celebrated in many Caribbean islands too. Some take place before Lent and some in August. None are as spectacular as Trinidad's. And those Carnivals started by Trinidadians living abroad do seem to be some of the most exciting outside the West Indies. As they say, nobody quite knows how to play mas like a Trinidadian!

▼ Some Trinidadians come to Toronto for the Caribana preparations and help design and construct some of the festival's spectacular costumes.

▲ During Caribana, thousands of people take the ferry to Toronto Island in Lake Ontario, to enjoy West Indian music, dancing, calypso singing, food and crafts.

The beautiful Carnival costumes have ▶ not been put away for very long before Trinidadians are thinking up spectacular ideas for next year's mas!

Caribana, Canada

One of the most exciting Carnivals apart from Trinidad's is Caribana in Toronto, Canada. Since it was first started by the West Indian community in 1967, it has got bigger and better every year. Toronto in February is often several feet deep in snow, which is not good weather for dancing in the streets! So, like Britain's Carnival celebrations, Caribana takes place on a public holiday in August. But it does take over most of the city centre, rather than being in just one district like Notting Hill.

A parade with as many as 13 masquerade bands and 3000 people in fancy dress winds through the city's main streets. It draws crowds of over 200 000 people. Live musical bands follow the masqueraders down to the Harborfront.

Toronto Island in Lake Ontario is completely taken over by West Indian art and craft exhibitions, dancing, concerts, calypso shows and food stalls. There are balls, floating nightclubs on the lake where steelbands play through the night, and a Children's Carnival.

There are more Trinidadians than other West Indians in Toronto.

Some say this explains Caribana's special excitement. And calypsonians, steelbands and costume designers from Trinidad come over to the city to help produce something of the dazzle and sparkle of their own mas. Caribana has become so popular that Toronto's hotels get fully booked for the festival. The West Indian community has given North America one of its most spectacular cultural celebrations.

The greatest show on earth

Many Trinidadians agree that Caribana's gaiety and excitement come closest to the spirit of their own festivities. But no one can beat the brilliance of their Carnival. The months of planning, designing, practising and rehearsing create an excitement which is unique. Finally it explodes into a few days of wild activity, colour and music which leaves the whole country exhausted by the morning of Ash Wednesday. Yet it is never very long before the band leaders, musicians and composers are once again plotting and working to make next year's Carnival the greatest show on Earth!

Acknowledgements

The author and publishers would like to thank Urvashi Butalia and Jeremy Taylor for their help in the preparation of this book and Sparrow Music for permission to publish the verse from the calypso 'Capatalism Gone Mad'.

The author and publishers wish to acknowledge the following photographic sources:
Caribbean Times, page 25
Alan Hutchinson Library, page 29
Ontario House, page 30 (2 photos)
Malta Government Tourist Office, page 28
Steve Rumney, pages 23 and 26
Paul Slattery, page 25
The remaining photographs used in this book were provided by the Commonwealth Institute.

First published 1986
Reprinted 1987, 1988

Published by
MACMILLAN EDUCATION LTD
Houndmills, Basingstoke, Hampshire RG21 2XS
and London
Companies and representatives
throughout the world

Designed by
The Tandem Design Company, Reading

Printed in Hong Kong

ISBN 0-333-37900-4

Index